Get Hired: The 21st Century Job Search

Finding the Job of Your Dreams

Dr. Ryan Anderson

To Cindy,
Best of luck on all
endeavors!
Sincerely,

Ryan Anderson

No Coast Consulting LLC

ISBN: 978-1-945663-19-2

Dedication

I dedicate this book to my family. I would like to especially thank my lovely wife, Lesley, for her unending support. Your patience and guidance helped make this book possible. My academic pursuits, including the writing of this book, haven't always been easy, but your commitment to our marriage and family has never waivered. I would also like to thank my parents, Mike and Sherri, for instilling in me a love of reading and life-long learning. I also dedicate this book to all my former students and coworkers who inspired me to write this book. May you find a job that aligns with your passion. This book is also dedicated to my two sons, Tobey and Grant. May you find your true calling in life! I can't wait to see how you positively impact the world. Enjoy the ride!

Contents

Acknowledgments

I would like to thank my family for reviewing this book prior to publication. I would also like to thank my many clients and students who motivated me to write this book. In addition, I would like to thank my friends and family who helped me stay motivated during the writing process.

I would like to express my gratitude to the many people who saw me through this book; to all those who provided support, talked things over, read, wrote, offered comments, allowed me to quote their remarks and assisted in the editing, proofreading, and design.

I would like to thank all who encouraged me during this process. Above all, I want to thank my wife, Lesley, and the rest of my family, who supported and encouraged me in spite of all the time it took me away from them. She had to sacrifice to make this project become a reality.

I would like to thank Deb Duncan for helping me in the process of content review and editing. Thanks to Bill Hansen for awesome art work on the book cover.

I would also like to thank all my wonderful colleagues at Grand View University. I never expected to be a business professor, but I truly love teaching. Every day I am thankful for the opportunity to pursue my passion. I am blessed to have found my calling.

I wrote this book to help you, the reader, land the job of your dreams. Use this book to develop a strategy to help you align your passion and your career. Following the process laid out in this book will help you land a career that is both emotionally and financially rewarding.

The Road Not Taken

BY ROBERT FROST

Two roads diverged in a yellow wood,
And sorry I could not travel both
And be one traveler, long I stood
And looked down one as far as I could
To where it bent in the undergrowth;

Then took the other, as just as fair,
And having perhaps the better claim,
Because it was grassy and wanted wear;
Though as for that the passing there
Had worn them really about the same,

And both that morning equally lay
In leaves no step had trodden black.
Oh, I kept the first for another day!
Yet knowing how way leads on to way,
I doubted if I should ever come back.

I shall be telling this with a sigh

Somewhere ages and ages hence:

Two roads diverged in a wood, and I—

I took the one less traveled by,

And that has made all the difference.

CHAPTER 1

Connect Your Passion to Your Career

"Opportunity is missed by most people because it is dressed in overalls and looks like work."

-Thomas Edison, Inventor and Businessman

Have you found yourself waking up every morning not wanting to go to work? Do you need help overcoming your fear of taking the plunge and searching for that next great opportunity? Do you struggle with where to start your job search? It has been my experience in the private sector and as a professor that many people are unhappy with their current jobs. I have had the honor of working for three Fortune 500 companies and also as a tenured business professor; in both professional contexts I have met many people who were unhappy with their professional lot in life. The reasons for their unhappiness are varied and far reaching: disagreements with the boss, bad cultural fit, or the employee's skill set and the tactical requirements of the job don't match. According to a recent Gallup.com workplace report, almost 70 percent of the U.S. workforce is not engaged at work. This amazing statistic has led to almost 300 billion dollars in lost productivity each year.[1]

Many employees leave their job because they don't get along with their boss. LaSalle Network recently conducted a survey of more than 1,000 people; 84 percent of respondents stated they've had a bad boss. Unfortunately, bad managers seem to fly under the radar; 55 percent stated they didn't report the bad manager to leadership.[2] Many employees are worried that if they speak up, they'll face serious consequences or be fired. This book provides some tips for people who are looking for a fresh start.

This book is designed to help the majority of Americans who are dissatisfied with their current professional situation. After accounting for sleep, we spend more time with our coworkers than we do with our friends and family. That is why it's critical to find a job that is both satisfying and pays the bills. This may sound like "Mission Impossible", but it is possible; I am a living, breathing example of this reality. My own professional trajectory took a non-linear path. My current job as a professor aligns with my worldview, but that hasn't always been the case. My own professional peaks and valleys have inspired me to write this book.

My Professional Story

Let me briefly share with you my personal story of professional trials and tribulations. I spent several years working in investments in the private sector in some great jobs, but none were meeting my sense of philanthropy. I found myself adding to corporate America's bottom line, but I wasn't meeting my sense of purpose. Instead, I made the mistake of chasing the money trail. While working for a Fortune 500 company I attended a professional conference in Santa Monica, California. I met an executive from a competing firm and we immediately hit it off. She spent the next five months recruiting me. I politely rebuffed her over many emails and lunches because at that time, I was pretty happy with my current job and organizational climate.

She called one morning and made a hard pitch. The conversation went something like this:

> *Vice President: "Ryan, let's stop doing this dance. What is it going to take to get you over to my company?" Then she did something very smart—she asked me about my current role: "What do you like about your current role and what could you live without?"*
>
> *Me: "I like this 80 percent of my current job…but could live without this 20 percent."*
>
> *Vice President: "What if I created a job that eliminated the portion you don't like and focused on what you enjoy? On top of that I will give you a 20 percent raise and a several thousand dollar signing bonus."*

I couldn't turn that offer down. The first week on the job she came up to me and told me she had taken an assignment with the company in Europe. I would no longer be reporting to her; instead I would be reporting to two other vice presidents. This whole situation shattered my trust because I had accepted the job assuming that I would be reporting directly to her. She withheld information knowing I would not accept the job if I knew she was leaving. Needless to say I was only in the role for a few months before quitting. This was a major lesson learned: always research the company and department prior to accepting a new role.

The definition of vocation is the blending of purpose and career. Over the last five years of career coaching and mentoring I was able to help many clients find new jobs and their vocations. My background in the private sector and as an educator allowed me to mentor many clients both formally and informally who were unhappy in their current career paths. Having completed both an M.B.A. and Ph.D. degrees, my strong academic background and hands-on professional experience has given me the skills and experience to help people find their long-term careers.

This book walks through some necessary steps to ensure that your next job is a success. The most important aspect of finding the right job is to be strategic in your job search. Reading this book will help you identify ways to find a job that will better align your purpose and passion with your paycheck.

The first part of this book is about using today's tools to find the right job including personal branding through social media, specifically using Glassdoor® and LinkedIn®, networking, and staying organized. The next section reviews crafting a resume, plus writing thank you notes for the 21st century job search. The third section of the book covers interview techniques; many behavioral-based questions stump people in the interview process. I provide tangible and strategic advice to help job searchers nail the difficult interview process. The final section of the book discusses career etiquette. It also includes a few tips on email follow up and correspondence.

My own experience of chasing a bigger paycheck was painful. It was the biggest professional mistake I'd made at that point in my young career. I didn't do my due diligence on the company or position. It is my hope that this book will help you avoid making the same mistakes.

The Difference Between Work and a Career

Many people assume that having a job and a career are the same thing. They are two very different words and approaches to how one makes a living. A lot of people are short sighted and search for a job instead of planning for the long haul and finding a career that can last a lifetime. According to Dictionary.com, *Job* is defined as the following:

1. A piece of work, especially a specific task done as part of the routine of one's occupation or for an agreed price.

2. A post of employment; full-time or part-time position.

3. Anything a person is expected or obliged to do; duty; responsibility.[3]

The definition of job focuses on the obligatory nature of work. In addition, it infers a transactional nature of the relationship between the employee and the employer: if you do this particular task we will pay this wage. Unfortunately, many people get locked into a lifetime of jumping from job to job partly because of the transactional way in which they pursue jobs.

On the other hand, finding a career can help you find a lifetime of happiness while also paying your bills. According to Dictionary.com, *Career* is defined as the following:

1. An occupation or profession, especially one requiring special training, followed as one's lifework.

2. A person's progress or general course of action through life or through a phase of life, as in some profession or undertaking.

3. Success in a profession, occupation, etc.[4]

The definition of a career infers that finding a career is an ongoing and transformational process. Finding a career is not something that lasts for only one or two positions, but situates you for a vocational trajectory that can last many decades.

In asking people why they work, I typically get the following replies:

1. To pay the bills

2. For food and clothes

3. Something to do

4. Self esteem

5. Familial or social expectations

None of the reasons listed above are guaranteed to help you find your career. In fact, most of the reasons listed above keep job searchers in a vicious transactional cycle going from position to position. My goal with this book is to help you find some tips and strategies that will help you find your career instead of just your next job.

This book will benefit those of you who are looking to change jobs or need some help strategizing about a career change. You will learn tips on the following items: cover letters, resumes, LinkedIn, interview techniques, and professional etiquette for follow-up communication. More specifically, you will discover essential techniques to finding the right cultural fit for your next job. After finishing this book, you will be able discover ways to find a better fit between your personal goals and ethos and your professional career track.

Each chapter in this book includes quotes and statistics related to the given topic of that chapter. At the end of each chapter are several discussion questions and exercises to recap the chapter's content.

After reading this book, you will be positioned to write an impactful resume, nail the interview, and follow up in a professional and expedient fashion, to ensure you are on the hiring manager's radar. It will help you align the tactical implementation of your job search with strategic best practices.

I have been blessed to coach and mentor many people from a variety of professional backgrounds and industries. I have mentored every level of employee from CFOs to customer service representatives. This book was written to provide a broad-based overview for the career search regardless of professional title or industry background.

I wish you nothing but the best as you engage with the content in this book. I hope you will find it useful in helping you become more purposeful with how you think about your career. I sincerely hope this book helps you find your life's purpose and vocation. Now onto Chapter 2...

CHAPTER 2

Technology and the 21st Century Job Search

"Treat your employees right, so they won't use your
Internet to search for a new job."

- Mark Zuckerberg, Founder of Facebook®

The 21st century job search is a complex maze of websites and
algorithms. To find the right job and company one must
search through the myriad of job boards and also conduct
online due diligence on prospective companies. The job
search is dramatically different than it was several years ago.
The old days of seeing an ad in the newspaper, applying in
person or at a career fair, and interviewing in person are long
gone. Today it's all about applicant tracking systems, applying
via Indeed®, LinkedIn, or some other online portal, and
teleconference interviews.

In the last ten years many job search websites (such as Indeed and Careerbuilder®) have become available to job seekers. Employers have increasingly relied on their websites and online application systems to hire employees. These sites make it easier for employers to reach applicants because they connect companies directly to aggregator websites that most candidates are now using. While job search websites have reduced cost and made it easier for hiring companies, they also create challenges for job seekers. Due to a job posting's unlimited virtual availability on the web, the number of people responding to online job postings has increased significantly.

This chapter discusses a few essential websites for today's job search including Google®, Indeed, Glassdoor, and LinkedIn. It also gives you some tips and tricks to help you make the most of what they have to offer.

Google

Google is one of the first places that recruiters turn to when considering candidates. Some recruiters use a simple Google search to find talent instead of paying for a background check. Some companies still do background checks, but many recruiters start with a simple Google search.

It takes two seconds for a recruiter to search your name and location. This means that the first page of your Google search results matters much more than it did before. The problem is that unlike a standard background check, what Google delivers on a name search isn't regulated. The user has very little control over what comes up.

So what can you do about this situation? First, become a publisher of your own content and flood Google with a lot of great keyword-rich content. If you are in a position to create your own website, all the better. Second, set up a Google alert with your name in quotations so you know every time a new job opening that meets your criteria shows up. This alert will help you track when prospective employers are looking into your background.

Indeed

Many people are familiar with Monster® and Careerbuilder, but not everyone is familiar with Indeed. I strongly recommend familiarizing yourself with Indeed.com, a job board aggregator that pulls job openings in from multiple sites. It's one of the most efficient tools when searching for jobs.

The first step in using Indeed is establishing your search queries. It's best to set up at least two job search queries in Indeed—one with more depth and one that is more explicit. For example, if you are looking for a financial analyst job in Chicago, Ill., the first search would use "analyst" for the keyword, no salary would be specified, and greater Chicago would be the target geographic region. The second search would use the exact job title you are searching for, narrow in on certain Chicago suburbs (for example Naperville or Schaumburg), and specify a certain salary range. This purpose of establishing at least two job queries will ensure that you don't miss out on any job openings.

Once you have established at least two queries in Indeed, log in at least once per day to check any jobs that have come into your organized list. Many people don't like getting more emails than they already do, but the occasional email going to your spam folder is worth receiving legitimate job openings during your job search.

The third step is to submit your job application via Indeed once you have located a job you are interested in. Many times the site redirects you to the job posting at the company's website. Occasionally you can submit your application directly through Indeed without any redirection. This is a weakness of Indeed; not every job can be applied for directly through their site. This may add some time to your job search since you might have to recreate an online profile at each individual company's human resources site.

It is not recommended to upload your resume to Indeed because you might be inundated by recruiters for sales positions, even if you are not in the sales field. Do not upload your resume to Indeed unless you are ready for a ton of cold calls and emails from recruiters who aren't always concerned with job fit.

Once you secure a new job you can unsubscribe from the daily emails and turn the queries off. If you are no longer interested in receiving additional emails from Indeed, close out your profile with them as well.

Glassdoor

Glassdoor has become a key component of today's job search process because using Glassdoor as a job seeker can set you above the competition. People who use Glassdoor for due diligence are both engaged and well researched. By providing insider information to prospective employees, this website has positively disrupted the job hunt. Glassdoor provides a variety of information about employers from employees' ratings to salary information to overall corporate information.

Here are some of the things you can research using Glassdoor.

- Employee Reviews

    Job searchers can use Glassdoor to review what current and past employees have to say about the company. Keep in mind that these reviews may provide a skewed sample of employees' feelings about the company culture. Employees who have a very strong negative or positive emotion about the company are generally more inclined to post on Glassdoor. That being said, don't immediately discount their comments. Look for overall trends in the comments about vacations, benefits, and company morale. According to a

2016 Glassdoor U.S. site survey, the majority of candidates read six reviews before forming an opinion about a company and 70 percent of people now look at reviews before they make career decisions.[5]

- Ratings System
    - In addition to written commentary by current and former employees, Glassdoor requires reviewers to rate the company using a five star system in five different areas: culture and values, work/life balance, senior management, compensation and benefits, and career opportunities.
    - According to a survey on RecruitingDaily.com about Glassdoor reviews, 30% of job seekers felt positive reviews in compensation and benefits were the most important. Benefits are

essential elements of what people look for before applying and interviewing at a company.[6]

- o A 2016 Glassdoor U.S. Site Survey shows that almost half of all job seekers over the last six months have taken Glassdoor reviews into consideration.[5] The most recent Glassdoor reviews factor into how job seekers perceive the company. Most job seekers review comments and ratings from the past six months.

Professional Branding

It's important to focus on building your professional brand. Anyone with a tablet, smart phone, or laptop can Google your name, so it's important that what they find is positive and polished. Recruiters love LinkedIn and Google. According to an article on RightManagement.ca,

"The savvy job seeker knows that if he is serious about finding a new job, he cannot ignore social media networking because recruiters are big on social recruiting. If you are a job seeker, social media allows you to broaden your network of contacts, and for LinkedIn in particular, it is a great way to reconnect with people with whom you lost contact. Broadening your network of contacts is also a way to learn about jobs before they are advertised."[7]

LinkedIn is a great social networking site for job seekers and also for professionals focused on doing their best in their current jobs. It is such a powerful tool that there is a whole chapter dedicated to LinkedIn later in this book.

Other social networks can also help you build and maintain your professional reputation; Google Plus is large and powerful and very well placed in Google search results. Wouldn't it be nice to have such an excellent professional reputation that your next job found you rather than the other way around? Don't lose out on a great opportunity prior to it being offered to you. In this day and age you and your personal brand are synonymous. It's imperative to have squeaky clean and positive search results when the recruiter researches your background via Google.

Having a strong and positive online presence can improve your brand and help attract employers' interest in you as a candidate. It is important to spend time and effort looking ahead to see what you might want to do next, plus you can better manage a smooth transition to that next phase in your career. Using online search tools like Glassdoor and Indeed can make you a more strategic job searcher. Glassdoor can help you better understand salary and cultural nuances with perspective employers. Indeed is a valuable online tool for casting the widest net when applying for jobs. Spending a few minutes Googling yourself is key to seeing what comes up so you can better understand what questions recruiters may have about you. Don't wait for a layoff or another life event that forces you into making a hasty move to something that may not be right for you. Be prepared by starting your research now.

Discussion Questions:

1. What can you do to improve your online brand?

2. What are the advantages of using Indeed versus individual job portals (i.e. Monster)?

3. What are some of the biggest changes in crafting a resume in today's job search?

4. How can Glassdoor be utilized to research potential employers?

Exercises:

1. On Glassdoor, research the top three companies you are interested in working for. Be sure to research both salary ranges and employee comments.

2. On LinkedIn, research best practices and create a profile to maximize your digital brand.

3. On Indeed establish a minimum of two job search queries. The first should focus on a very limited

geographic and keyword search. The second query
should be broad based.

4. Customize your resume for each job opening.
   Chapter 5 will cover details on how to best
   maximize your resume.

CHAPTER 3

Networking and the Job Search

"Best results are often achieved well before you need a job, by consistently networking so that when you find yourself job-hunting you have a large network to work with."
-Erik Qualman, Author and Motivational Speaker

In today's dynamic and challenging job market it's important to have a strong network of people who can help you identify job opportunities. Networking will be a key component in finding a job. According to an article on LinkedIn.com, "…85% of critical jobs are filled via networking of some sort; being highly networked is essential for both the job seekers and for those seeking them."[8]

Most people inherently know that a job search coupled with effective networking can get a job faster than a job search with no networking. Networking enables you to access exponentially more job opportunities! A warm job lead is worth a dozen cold job openings. Having an inside track at a company where there is an opening is key to landing that position; an internal reference gives you a leg up on the competition. Networking is a strategy to uncover more job opportunities. It is a way of connecting with others, including people you know and new people you've never met before. People are wired to both connect with and help others. Many people in your network can and will open professional doors for you if they know you are looking for a job.

Networking is simply investing time in getting to know people. Most people are not aware that they are networking every day. You are networking when you strike up a conversation with the person at the grocery store, introduce yourself to other parents at your child's t-ball game, meet a friend for coffee, catch up with a former co-worker, or stop to chat with your neighbor. When you are on a job search every person you meet and interact with could be a potential referral for your next job. People tend to do business with people they already know and like so if you already have an established relationship with a person, they are more likely to recommend you for a job opening. It may surprise you to know that the job you want may not be advertised at all. Active networking creates job leads frequently before a formal job description is created or a job is announced. You can often find out about a job through networking before the job is officially posted.

Networking has changed dramatically over the last few years. Here are some tips on how to effectively use and expand your network.

Why Networking is so Important
for Landing a Job

Trying to find a job without networking is like trying to fish without bait. The statistics don't lie when it comes to how many people have landed a job through networking.

"Networking can help you get hired and help you grow your career. LinkedIn reports:

- 70 percent of people in 2016 were hired at a company where they had a connection.

- 80 percent of professionals consider professional networking to be important to career success.

- 35 percent of surveyed professionals say that a casual conversation on LinkedIn Messaging has led to a new opportunity.

- 61 percent of professionals agree that regular online interaction with their professional network can lead the way to possible job opportunities."[9]

Networking Dos and Don'ts

The key to successful networking is putting aside unrealistic expectations about networking. Rome wasn't built in a day and it takes time to establish contact with people. Do not pursue networking like it's a one-time business transaction; it's important to have the long game in mind. Set realistic expectations for how long it takes to get warm leads from your network. See below for a list of networking dos and don'ts.

- Do invest sufficient time in networking. The more time you invest in it, the better you will become at it.

- Don't be absent. The only way to truly fail at networking is to not show up.

- Do be determined. Networking is a continual process that rewards persistence.

- Don't think networking is a quick fix. Networking is not an immediate guarantee of job search success.

- Do make networking something you do every day. Networking, like sales, is truly a lifestyle; you need to commit time and money to see effective results.

- Don't wait to start networking until it's too late. Networking is not something you should do only after you have lost a job.

- Do network to find a job. Networking is something that you can do to increase the likelihood of getting a job.

- Do be prepared when networking. Always bring a notebook, a pen, your business cards, and your best game face.

- Don't come unprepared. Do some research about who may be attending any networking event.

- Do prepare a 30-second elevator pitch. You need a short speech that succinctly sells the best possible version of who you are professionally.

- Don't network without first reflecting on your strengths, desires, and goals, plus develop a heightened sense of self-awareness. It is important to know how to sell your strengths and weaknesses to everyone, especially prospective employers.

Developing a Networking Strategy

It is critical to be strategic about your job search. Develop a networking strategy that includes a good elevator pitch; it is key to nailing the networking circuit. Your elevator speech should explain what you do, what you like and dislike, where you're coming from, plus you need to practice, practice, and practice that speech. Attend monthly networking events, especially professional or community groups that will help you build relationships via their monthly meetings.

Networking should not be done without a deliberate plan. It's important to capture your best qualities in a concise format, but you should also focus on your natural markets—those that are closest to you. If you are a young professional, seek out civic groups organized around your age group like Young Professionals. If you are an accountant, seek out groups focused on the accounting industry. According to an article in *U.S. News & World Report*, "Prepare your elevator speech explaining who you are and what you do, and practice enough that you sound like a natural. Schedule at least two or three events a month, and find groups that you want to join so that you build relationships through the monthly meetings."[10]

Don't approach networking like speed dating. Always take a quantity of business cards to events, but don't just quickly walk through the room collecting and handing out business cards. It's important to be sincere in how you approach people when networking. Spend time with everyone you meet and ask leading questions of the people you interact with, so you truly get to know them. People can sense the insincere networkers who are just there to work the room. According to an article, "Have a stack of business cards ready to hand out. You don't want to be the person who works the room racing to collect and hand out your cards, though. Save the exchange for when you have a conversation. People can sense greedy networkers who are there to work the room and add as many contacts to their mailing list without permission."[10]

Start With Your Key Supporters–
Your References

When tapping into your network it's important to start with the people you use as references, people who already like you and can endorse your knowledge, skills, and abilities. References have already agreed to put in a good word for you with a prospective employer. According to an article on LinkedIn.com, "Job seekers need to realize networking is not trying to meet as many people as possible. It's about meeting a few well-connected people who can vouch for your ability and who are willing to refer you to a few other well-connected people."[8] These people are also more likely to provide a warm lead when it comes to job openings. Here are some tips when contacting your references.

- Contact each one of your references individually about grabbing coffee or lunch.

- Be very candid about your reason for reaching out to them, including describing your goals for the job search.

- Keep them informed on your job search progress.

- Prepare them for any calls or email requests from prospective employers.

Networking Events

Many people assume that digital networking is the only way to connect with people in today's technologically-oriented society. Meeting people in person for coffee or lunch can carry a lot of weight. In addition, almost every size community will have a variety of networking events and community groups you can join; take time to locate them. According to a LinkedIn article, "If you belong to a professional association, attend a meeting or a mixer. You'll find that many of the participants have the same goals you do and will be glad to exchange business cards. If your college alma mater holds alumni networking events (many schools hold them at locations across the country) be sure to attend."[11]

Laundry List

You know more people than you think. You don't have to be a member of ten networking groups to develop a good-sized network. Keep in mind your network includes your family members, friends, neighbors, co-workers, and colleagues. Start going through your social media and cell phone contacts and compile a list of prospects who might be able to assist you in a job search. It's amazing how fast your list grows.

Think of your network as overlapping concentric circles. The more people you know, the more common connections you will have. In fact, you already belong to many informal networks including community groups, professional organizations, church, friends, and family. Each network connects you to another network. For example, your child's teacher can connect you with other parents, schools, and school suppliers.

Connect With Your Network

It doesn't matter how big your network is if no one knows you are on a job search. Once you've developed your list of contacts, start reaching out to the people in your network. Let them know that you're looking for a job. Be specific about what kind of job titles and companies you are interested in. Don't make assumptions that people won't be willing to open up their rolodex to assist you in the job search. You may be surprised by who they know and what they'll do to help you.

Don't be shy about asking for help on the job search. In general, people like to give advice and be recognized for their expertise. Almost everyone has been on the other side of the unemployment aisle—they know what it feels like to be out of work. Connecting with people can be invigorating and rewarding, for both extroverts and introverts.

The first step is to set up meetings or interviews with select individuals who are in the best position to help you achieve your professional goals. During these informational interviews learn about their roles, obtain valuable industry advice, and, most importantly, ask them for referrals to other individuals who can help you out. You simply want them to share their knowledge with you, to set you in the right direction on your career search.

Have the Long Game in Mind

It's important to be authentic when networking. If you look immediately for what you can get out of a relationship, you are likely to only build short-term, unsatisfactory relationships. Be genuine when you are interacting with people in your network, be interested in how you can help them, and view those network relationships as long-term commitments.

Ask for advice, not a job. If you ask directly for a job, it will come off as one sided and too aggressive. You want your networking contacts to become advocates in your job search, but don't make them feel captive or mandated to do so. Don't let one of the first key moments you have in building a relationship revolve around the request for a job. Be sure to ask what they are comfortable with in terms of helping you.

Be Specific in Your Request

When asking for help with a job search it is important to be explicit in your request for help. Do some due diligence to know exactly how the contact may help you prior to making the request. Do you need a reference? Does the contact have a specific in with a particular company or industry? Are you looking for a referral? Do you need to conduct an informational interview to learn more about the industry? The key to networking is being both authentic and specific in your request. Here is a sample job search networking request.

Contact Name, Title
Company
Address
City, State, Zip

Dear Mr. Contact Name,

I was referred to you by Diane Smithers from XYZ Company in New York. She recommended you as an excellent source of information on the communications industry.

My goal is to secure an entry-level position in communications. I would appreciate hearing your advice on career opportunities in the communications industry, on conducting an effective job search, and on how best to uncover job leads.

Thanks so much in advance for any insight and advice you would be willing to share. I look forward to contacting you early next week to set up a telephone informational interview.

Sincerely,
First Name Last Name

Prioritize Your Networks

Establishing who is most important in your network is the key to maintaining it. Being able to allocate time to cultivating your most important contacts is critical. Maintaining your professional network is just as important as building it, so take time to nurture those relationships. Having more contacts isn't necessarily better; the key is quality, rather than quantity. Focus on cultivating and maintaining your existing network; you're sure to discover an incredible array of information, knowledge, expertise, and opportunities if you invest the time to get to know your networking contacts better.

List the people who are crucial to your network and try to connect with them each quarter at a minimum. Keep a running list of people you need to reconnect with; if you haven't seen them in a while, reconnect and then schedule a regular meeting or phone call. After that, keep a running list of your second tier contacts. Prioritize these contacts and then schedule time into your regular routine so you can make your way down the list. It's important to schedule time for both reaching out and meeting with each contact at least once a year.

Don't be a hit-and-run networker: connecting, getting what you want, and then disappearing, never to be heard from until the next time you need something. Invest in your network by following up and providing feedback to those who were kind enough to offer their help. Thank them for their referral and assistance and tell them whether you got the interview or the job. If you didn't get either, report on the lack of success and ask for additional help.

Being able to prioritize your natural base of contacts will help you know when and how to reach out to your network. When networking it is important to be sincere, prepared, and respectful. Be up front with people about your intentions. Don't be overbearing with your request; if people aren't receptive to your inquiry, politely thank them and move on. Sometimes the most important aspect of networking is knowing how to gracefully accept a "no thank you".

Networking is the key to landing a job in today's competitive job search. Anything you can do to stand out against the sea of job-seeking competitors can help you get the job you want. Most jobs come through personal connections. Building your network in an authentic and ethical way should be a top priority when you are searching for your next professional opportunity.

Discussion Questions:

1. What is the appropriate way to let your contacts know you are on a job search?

2. How should you prioritize your contact list?

3. Why is it so important to be specific in your request for an informational interview?

4. Why should you start with your references?

Exercises:

1. Research five dos and don'ts of networking.

2. Create and practice your elevator pitch.

3. Track down five networking events or groups to check out.

4. Write down notes after the networking event to ensure when you follow up with people you can personalize your correspondence.

CHAPTER 4

Staying Organized

"Choose a job you love, and you will never have to
work a day in your life."

–*Confucius, Chinese teacher, editor, politician, and philosopher*

Finding a job can be one of the most frustrating and time-consuming processes you will undergo. I have found that most people wait until it's too late to engage in the job search—they wait until they have lost a job and so may not be in the best emotional state to dedicate passion and energy to a job search. The process of finding a job requires a consistent level of engagement. It's easy to get disillusioned when you receive "Dear John" letters from hiring managers. Emotionally, the process can be draining. This chapter provides you with tips on how to close the deal on finding that next job, and ways to stay organized during the search.

In today's job market it's not uncommon to apply for many positions. That involves a great deal of time and energy. You don't want to waste precious hours by missing important application deadlines, inverting companies and positions, confusing interview times, or forgetting to follow up. Here are some tips on how to stay organized during the job search.

Develop a System

You'll need to develop strategies to monitor the positions you've applied for and the status of each application. Tracking is especially important for following up with employers. Monitor where employers are in the process and then track that information so you can make a follow-up phone call or email in a timely manner. Many systems are possible; find the one that works best for you. The most widely used is a Microsoft Excel spreadsheet. You could also use a Microsoft Word document to track progress; whatever works best for you. See below for detailed suggestions.

Create an Excel Spreadsheet

If you're familiar with Microsoft Excel or a similar program, creating a spreadsheet is a simple and effective way to keep track of your job applications. Utilize the following column headers within the spreadsheet:

- **Company Name**—The name of the organization you're applying to.

- **Contact**—Your point of contact at the company (who you addressed your cover letter to, such as a Director of Human Resources or Office Manager).

- **Email**—The email address of your point of contact.

- **Phone Number**—If you have it, add the point of contact's phone number.

- **Date Applied**—The date you submitted your application.

- **Application Summary**—What you submitted: a cover letter, resume, and any corresponding documents.

- **Interview**—The date and time your interview is scheduled.

- **Follow-Up Date**—Identify a date to follow up with the interviewer.

- **Follow-Up**—Indicate how you followed up.

- **Status**—If you were rejected, offered the job, asked in for a second interview, etc.

Gmail Account and Google Calendar

It's easiest to stay organized when you have a dedicated email account for your job search. If you like to stay organized online, Google is a great way to go and Gmail is great for opening a new email account. The advantage of using Google is that you can link your Gmail account to Google Drive and Google Calendar. You can use Google Drive to create, save, and export documents like your resume and cover letter. You can also link up with Google Calendar to stay on top of important dates, including interviews and follow-up reminders.

Research Organizations

If you focus your job search on a dozen or so top tier employers you can funnel your job search. Where do you want to work? Start with a list of 20 to 25 organizations that you consider ideal to work for and narrow it down to 10 to 15. Research to see if you know any people who are working, or have worked, at any of these employers. If so, send an email to that contact requesting an informational interview to learn more about the company's culture. After that, set up automated job queries on your top tier employers for job openings that match your criteria.

Carve Out Time Each Day for Your Job Search

It's important to commit to a certain block of time every day to work on your job search. Searching for a new position is a job in itself and it's important to approach it as such. The amount of time you allocate to your job search directly impacts the speed of landing a new job. I would recommend allocating at least four hours each day to applying for jobs.

The environment you are in while searching for jobs is also critical to finding a job. It's easy to get distracted if you stay at home. If possible, go to a local coffee shop or library instead. If you do stay home, an office set up or other quiet space is needed when applying for jobs, to avoid distractions.

Establishing your job search process is an important part of finding your next job. Staying organized and using project management tools greatly increases the likelihood of quickly landing a high-quality job. Developing a system, using technology, and researching companies in a targeted manner can make your job search more efficient and effective.

Discussion Questions:

1. What kind of tools should you use to organize your job search?

2. How should you prioritize your targeted company list?

3. Why is it so important to request an informational interview with a contact at one of your target companies?

4. How should you approach your job search?

Exercises:

1. Research twenty companies you would like to work for.

2. Track all job applications in an Excel spreadsheet or using a similar program.

3. Develop your job search system, including establishing a calendar and follow-up process.

4. Write down notes after you complete some informational interviews with your contacts.

CHAPTER 5

The Contemporary Resume - Strategies and Tips

"The challenge of life, I have found, is to build a resume that doesn't simply tell a story about what you want to be, but it's a story about who you want to be."

- Oprah Winfrey, Talk Show Host, Actress, Producer, and Philanthropist

The 21st century job search is challenging. To start overcoming employer entry barriers make sure you have a high-quality resume that matches each specific job description. This chapter focuses on what it takes to have a high-profile resume in today's cutthroat business world. It reviews current methods and strategies for formulating the best resume based on today's hyper-competitive job market. Chapter 6 covers the mechanics and logistics of resume writing. This chapter covers topics such as analyzing transferrable skill sets, customizing your resume, accomplishments versus duties, explaining gaps in employment, and using action verbs.

Action Verbs

Using appropriate verbs is critical to catching the eye of a recruiter. According to a study released by TheLadders.com, an online job-matching service, recruiters spend an average of six seconds reviewing an individual resume.[12] The total time that recruiters spend on the whole document is less than a minute. You must use strong and appropriate verbs to grab their attention.

The problem with most resumes is that applicants use bland action words when crafting their resume. The verbs used are neither exciting nor descriptive. To combat this problem, use a list of action verbs or a thesaurus. Try to match up action words in your resume with keywords from the job description you are applying for. The next chapter contains a list of specifically-recommended verbs to incorporate into your resume.

Transferrable Skill Sets

Today's job openings require a breadth of skills. Many times folks doing a job search feel obligated to stay in their current industry. The 21st century job search does not have explicit rules about only applying for openings in your current industries. That doesn't mean you shouldn't start the job search in your current industry; it simply means don't limit your search to your current industry. Knowing how to highlight transferable skills can make all the difference in your job search.

If you're changing fields and feeling a little under qualified, you can use transferable skills to get a hiring manager to take a chance on you. According to an article on TheMuse.com, the following simple equation can help decipher if a skill set is considered transferable.

"To figure out if something is a transferable skill worth mentioning, use this formula:

"As a [prior role], I [explain a responsibility], which taught me [transferable skills]. That's a skill I would draw on from day one as a [new role]."[13]

This simple and easy-to-use equation can help you determine how to best market your transferrable skill sets. Examples from TheMuse.com article:

"As a volunteer coordinator, I managed 150 people across three cities. It taught me how to keep a large group motivated, on task, and moving toward larger goals. That's a skill I would draw on from day one in this management role.

"As a [side gig title], I was also responsible for all of the processes that made my venture possible. It taught me next-level organization, as well as to be responsible for scheduling and invoicing, which are skills I would draw on from day one in this operations role."[13]

Once you have drafted a few examples for your resume or cover letter, you are in great shape to start the application. Be sure to review appropriate buzzwords from the job description and incorporate them into your narrative if at all possible. The bullet points you draft should clearly establish that you are a lifelong learner and have the skills the employer is looking for.

Accomplishments versus Duties

Many people use the "low hanging fruit" approach when it comes to completing a resume. They focus on the tactical aspects of their job, but not the large accomplishments they have achieved. It's easy to slip into this mode where you simply start listing job duties on your resume; don't do this. Instead, make your accomplishments as quantitative as possible by using hard numbers to accentuate your achievements. Here are some examples of a resume's bullet points that simply list job duties.

- Trained all customer service staff on company policies and procedures.

- Responsible for personnel training and evaluation.

- Updated departmental files.

Employers don't care as much about your daily tasks as what you've accomplished. They are looking for statements more like those listed below.

- Responsible for the systematic training of 100 high-performing customer service staff, which led to a ten percent reduction in training costs.

- Revised the onboarding process for new employees, which saved 100 hours of training time per year.

- Reorganized ten years' worth of unwieldy files, making them easily accessible to all department members.

The process of organizing your resume to focus on achievements versus tasks will help you directly answer the most important question that a prospective employer has: What problem can the candidate help me solve? It puts your accomplishments in black and white. It is all right to list the most critical duties of your previous work experience, but do not simply list your day-in and day-out laundry list of tasks.

Customized Resumes

Several years ago a more generic resume was fine; it didn't matter whether your resume was geared toward a particular company. This one-size-fits-all approach is no longer effective. If you use this approach for all employers your resume will most likely end up in a recycle bin. Thanks to the Internet, you—and employers—have access to more information and you must show them how and why you fit the position they are advertising.

Today's recruiters have higher and more specific expectations when it comes to your resume. Sending off a few targeted resumes is a much better strategy than sending out many general ones. Focus on customizing each resume and cover letter for the company that you're targeting, using two specific actions. (1) Review the job description for key buzzwords. Applicant Tracking Systems will use the same words to screen candidates in and out of the job search. The professional summary and core competencies section of your resume should be modifiable. Chapter 6 discusses this process in further detail. (2) Adjust your cover letter based on each job's qualifications and requirements section. These typically include words or phrases that you see repeatedly in a job posting, or listed under qualifications or requirements. Do not use synonyms for these words or phrases; Applicant Tracking Systems are programmed to catch the exact words or phrases employers are looking for. Perform this check every time you apply for a job. You may think it's clear in your resume that you possess those skills, but you need to carefully cross reference it with each job posting and identify the most used action words or catch phrases.

According to an article in *U.S. News & World Report*, "In the past, you could simply list your duties on your resume for each position, basically mirroring your actual job description. This no longer works. Instead of stating your past, you need to take the employer's viewpoint. What about your work would they be most interested in? Focusing on the company's perspective allows you to demonstrate what you can do for them, which is what they care about."[14] Remember, every opportunity requires a customized resume.

Relationships Trump Resumes

Having the best resume is just a start in securing a job. It's all about who you know. Networking, both online via LinkedIn and face to face, is essential to securing that next job. Thanks to the popularity of social media, your resume may not be the first thing a potential employer sees about you. As more people connect with each other on social media sites, a potential employer is far more likely to see your social media online profile before ever setting eyes on your resume. Shift your priorities from, "I have to update my resume!" to "How can I expand my network?"

Gaps in Employment

Large gaps in your resume aren't as important as they used to be. Not only do employers realize that wonderful people get laid off, but they also appreciate when candidates show initiative and volunteer, take a temp job, or try to start their own business. That being said, when a candidate is applying for a job, a large, unexplained gap in his or her employment history is sometimes a showstopper. It's important to show progression, not status quo, over the trajectory of your career. A long employment gap can suggest the opposite of that. It's important to acknowledge gaps in employment.

According to an article in *U.S. News & World Report*, when it comes to gaps in unemployment, "While these are no longer uncommon, you need to be transparent. If it's not apparent why there is a big gap in your work history, you should consider how to address it because an employer may just move on...Give them the information. You don't need to go into excruciatingly personal detail, but it's a good idea to address layoffs if you've had a series of them and personal issues that have resulted in work gaps."[14]

Here are a few tips for how to successfully address gaps in employment.

1. If you left a job voluntarily, don't be afraid to mention why.

   It's perfectly okay to mention sabbaticals: the year you took off to travel the world or to take care of a family situation. If there's a purpose associated with that gap, it's much more acceptable to hiring managers than a generic gap that just looks like you were being lazy. For example you could say, "I took two years off to complete my college degree, or my spouse was sick and I needed to stay home to take care of him/her." These explanations are much more acceptable than, "I didn't feel like working for two years."

2. <u>Emphasize any activities you undertook during the time gap to improve your professional standing.</u>
   Be sure to list any certifications or college courses you completed during the time gap. If you've done any consulting or contract work, be sure to bring that up. Include any other valuable experiences, including volunteering or major personal projects.

3. <u>Be Honest.</u>
   Honesty is the best policy when it comes to addressing gaps in employment. If you explain gaps in your employment history on your resume, it shows the hiring manager or recruiter that you have continuity in your career. In today's volatile job market it is not unheard of to change jobs every few

years. According to an article on thebalance.com, "Many workers spend five years or less in every job, so they devote more time and energy transitioning from one job to another."[15] That being said, you still need to justify any gaps in your employment.

Specificity

Bullet points used in resumes should be specific. A lot of job searchers use vague or broad language, which is not good enough. Prospective employers need to understand what you've achieved in your previous work experience. Here are some examples of the difference between vague responses and more specific alternatives.

A. Worked with employees in a retail setting.

B. Hired, trained, and supervised more than ten employees in the retail sector, with one million dollars in annual sales.

Both of these phrases could easily describe the same person, but the details and specifics in example B will more likely grab an employer's attention. The specificity of bullet points and related skill sets is an essential part of getting the attention of prospective recruiters.

Cover Letters: A Thing of the Past?

Many people wonder if cover letters need to be submitted with resumes. If this book was written five to ten years ago a whole chapter would have been dedicated just to the topic of cover letters, but things have quickly changed. Cover letters become less important each year. The resume, with a good, professional summary, provides much of the same information as a cover letter. According to a *Forbes* article, "...90% of hiring managers admit that they never even read cover letters."[16] LinkedIn and other social media outlets tell us what the cover letter won't. The article in *Forbes* maintains, "Today, 80% of jobs never get publicly posted and 80% of jobs are acquired through networking. Needless to say, those numbers underscore the scarcity of the cover letter in today's job hunt."[16] Social media gives us more access to each other's lives, making cover letters less necessary. LinkedIn and other online tools have negated the necessity of the cover letter and hard copy resume.

The most imperative part of writing a high-quality resume isn't always the mechanics and nuts and bolts, sometimes it's the strategy you set and the framework in which you write your document. Crafting a good resume reflects your best technical and interpersonal skills to a prospective employer. According to Dan Miller, the author of *48 Days To The Work You Love*, a recent Yale University study reported that 15 percent of the reason for a person's success is due to technical skill and knowledge, and 85 percent of the reason originates from the person's personal skill: attitude, enthusiasm, self-discipline, desire, and ambition."[17]

Being able to accurately describe your interpersonal skills on the resume is a very important part of landing the interview. Knowing a few basic rules for resume writing can keep you from making some critical mistakes while you are on a job search. The best resume strategy involves the following items: focusing on transferable skill sets, explaining gaps in employment, listing achievements instead of duties, customizing your document for each position, and specifically listing your accomplishments. Following these points is critical to successfully landing that next job.

Discussion Questions:

1. What should you focus on when searching a prospective job description?

2. Why is it important to use specificity in your resume?

3. Why is it essential to use the right kind of verbs at the start of each bullet point when listing your professional experience?

4. How should you explain time gaps in employment?

Exercises:

1. Research three job openings and customize your resume based on the keywords and required skills for those positions.

2. Take at least two bullet points from each position and quantify them with specific data.

3. Research the most commonly-used verbs and action words to make sure your resume has a variety of words at the start of each bullet point.

4. Write down two large accomplishments for each position you have held.

CHAPTER 6

The Contemporary Resume – Structure and Tactical Rules

"The internet was supposed to make this whole business of job searching rational and simple. You could post your resume and companies would search them and they'd find you. It doesn't seem to work that way. There aren't enough jobs for experienced, college educated managers and professionals."

- Barbara Ehrenreich, Author

Completing a top tier resume is one part strategy and one part tactical implementation. Chapter 5 focused on the strategy behind a good resume. This chapter focuses on the specific action items to execute for a fantastic resume. The art of resume writing has changed a lot over the years. The content contained below will highlight some cutting-edge tips to ensure that your resume is polished and of the highest quality. A top tier resume is not only mechanically correct and free of spelling and punctuation errors, but also includes a compelling objective statement and a core competencies section.

The New Objective Statement

Every resume used to contain an objective statement that would promote the kind of culture and workplace you were looking for, as well as what kind of job you were looking for. Employers already know what kind of position you are looking for because they have your application. The bottom line is that employers don't care what you are looking for; they care about your skills and if your personality is a good cultural fit for their organization.

Today's resume must include a professional summary. This is a four-to-six-sentence paragraph that touts your top skills and achievements. The paragraph focuses on your last one or two positions and summarizes the bullet points from the professional experience section.

When crafting your professional summary section, it is important to use specific language that speaks to the job posting. Employers read your professional summary section, but too often they skip quickly past vague pufferies like, "Seeking a challenging position that offers professional growth." Give employers something specific and, more importantly, something that focuses on their needs as well as your own. For example, "A challenging entry-level marketing position that allows me to contribute my skills and experience in fundraising for non-profits." See below for an example of a professional summary.

Leading process management professional involved in delivering high-quality enterprise-wide solutions and analytics. A manager with the exceptional ability to identify and resolve complex problems through collaborative communication with a wide variety of departments and clients. Strong reputation for cross-functional leadership working in highly complex and large organizations. Excellent record of successfully completing multiple projects at the same time and ahead of schedule. Able to motivate a workforce to sustain high levels of productivity and accomplish challenging goals. Results-oriented general manager with extensive experience in Fortune 500 companies as well as start-ups. Established service management strategy for a multi-million dollar organization.

Core Competencies Section

This section follows the professional summary in the body of the resume and should include nine to twelve of your top skills. This section contains adjectives and generally is formatted in three vertical columns and three or four rows. It should be modifiable based on the keywords and required skills listed in the job description. These skills should include your most widely-used action words. See the example below of a core competencies section.

Project Management	Personnel Oversight	Total Quality Management
Data Quality Control	Lean/Continuous Improvement	Root Cause Analysis
Process Improvement	Six Sigma	Service Management

Length

Once upon a time, recruiters said that resumes should never exceed one page. It didn't matter if someone had one or ten years of experience; they expected everyone to fit everything on one page. The reason for a short resume was that recruiters spent so little time actually reading it. According to an article in the *U.S. News & World Report*, "Employers are spending little time reviewing resumes nowadays. Since many companies cut personnel to save on costs, hiring managers and human resources departments have less time these days. This has increased workloads, which sometimes pushes the hiring process farther down the list of priorities. Because of that, you have about 30 seconds to make an impression on your resume."[14] The resume must also show your professional highlights in a very concise manner. "Whatever the length of the resume, the critical factor is to make absolutely certain that your reader's interest is piqued within the first half of the first page," cautions Laurie J. Smith, president of Creative Keystrokes Executive Resume Service.[18]

Today's standard for a resume is one to two pages, depending on the level and length of experience. In general, the two-page resume is now taking the place of the initial screening interview. Grant Cooper of Strategic Resumes offers this view of the two-page resume, "The resume has now taken the place of the initial interview, and only those with significant qualifications and strong resumes are even invited to interview. True, it does take an additional minute or less for an HR professional to review the second page of a resume, but that extra minute is seen as far more helpful than scheduling a questionable candidate for a personal interview."[18] See below for some general guidelines related to the appropriate length of the resume.

- Resumes for new graduates and entry-level job seekers are often, but not always, one page.

- A two-page resume is the best bet for the vast majority of job seekers.

- No matter what the length, the resume must be concise and capture attention on the first page, and preferably the first third of the first page.

Action Verbs

Use action verbs to describe your skills and accomplishments when writing your resume and cover letters. These powerful words help demonstrate your strengths as an employee and highlight why you are right for that particular job.

Many hiring managers quickly skim through all the resumes and cover letters they receive. The average hiring manager spends only about ten seconds per resume, so it is critical that you use strong verbs to accentuate your skills. These action verbs should jump off your page, quickly showing the hiring manager that you have the skills and other qualifications for the job. In addition, because employers read so many job applications, the language gets repetitive and boring. If your words are the same as everyone else's, it will be hard for you to stand out.

Action words can help with the flow of your resume; they make it easier for you to connect one point to the next. The goal of every resume should be to make sure that each and every bullet leads nicely into the next one. Action verbs have a certain power to them that other words do not. They can place emphasis points in the appropriate place, so take the time to select them carefully.

Some examples of action verbs include accomplished, designed, initiated, and supervised. Try to avoid using phrases like "responsible for". Instead, craft a bullet point with action verbs like this one: "Resolved user questions as part of an IT help desk serving 4,000 students and staff." Here is a list of action verbs.

Accomplish	Direct	Integrate	Represent
Analyze	Encourage	Manage	Research
Apply	Enforce	Perform	Use
Approve	Initiate	Persuade	Validate
Coach	Innovate	Plan	Collaborate
Inspire	Perform	Coordinate	Install
Report	Resolve		

Typos and Grammatical Errors

Your resume needs to be grammatically and mechanically perfect. If it isn't, employers will read between the lines and draw not-so-flattering conclusions about you like, "This person can't write," or "This person obviously doesn't care." These basic tactical errors can kill your prospects with a hiring manager. You know how to spell just fine, but you've stared at your resume for so many hours that it almost seems like a different language to you. It's easy to miss a typo or grammatical error.

It's not enough to use spell check to catch the obvious errors. The easiest way to combat simple spelling errors is to have someone else review your resume. For many people, spelling mistakes and grammar issues leap off the page and a second opinion can be invaluable for your resume. Here are a few ways to avoid typos.

- Have a trusted friend or partner read through your resume.

- Reread your leading verbs and eliminate duplicates.

- Edit your content in sections.

- Double check your hyperlinks to ensure they are valid.

References

A list of references is a group of people who the employer might contact to learn more about your professional qualifications. They can be a former boss or co-worker. These people should be able to vouch for your qualifications for a job. Sometimes an employer will contact only one person on the list, and other times they will contact everyone. The employer might reach out to these references either via email or phone.

It is a best practice to not include references in your resume. Since you should limit your resume to one or two pages, it's important to not waste valuable space by listing references in the resume document. Generally, references are provided only upon request, and when they are, they're added in a separate document.

There are a few instances when you can include references in your resume. If a job listing specifically requests references, include them. Put them in a separate document, providing each reference's name, title, company, address, email, and phone number. Here is what a sample reference could look like.

Jane Doe

Human Resources Manager

ABC Company

Address

City, State ZIP Code

Phone

Email

Putting together a top tier resume involves a very explicit and formalized process. It entails making sure that you have no more than two pages, no spelling or grammatical errors, and includes both a core competencies and a professional summary section. The resume should not include your references within the document; they should be listed in a separate document and only if specifically requested. By reviewing and implementing the tips from Chapters 5 and 6 of this book you should be able to put together a high-quality resume that gets the attention of recruiters.

Discussion Questions:

1. What should you focus on when organizing your resume?

2. Why is it important to use action verbs in your resume?

3. Why is it important to place your references in a separate document?

4. How can you avoid typos and other mechanical errors?

Exercises:

1. Create a list of your top twelve professional skills.

2. Create a professional summary that provides a high-level overview of your professional accomplishments.

3. Identify the ten most common action verbs for your industry and the position you are seeking.

4. Create a reference document with three of your best professional references from past and current co-workers and supervisors.

CHAPTER 7

The Art of LinkedIn™

"Your LinkedIn profile must be consistent with how you portray yourself elsewhere. Not only should your official résumé match the experience you list on LinkedIn, but it also should be consistent with Twitter and public Facebook information."

-Melanie Pinola, Author of LinkedIn in 30 Minutes: How to create a rock-solid LinkedIn profile and build connections that matter

The 21ˢᵗ century job search revolves around creating a top tier LinkedIn profile, which is a digital showcase for anyone looking for a promotion or new job. LinkedIn is no longer an optional job search tool; if you are looking for a job, you need to have a fully-developed LinkedIn profile. This profile isn't just a digitized version of your resume; it's a place to showcase your best assets and successes. If you're like more than 450 million others on the planet, you're going to let LinkedIn do the heavy lifting of finding a new position. Not only are more and more individuals placing their professional profiles up on LinkedIn, but more organizations are using it for recruiting purposes. Many businesses are using LinkedIn as either their primary, or in many cases exclusive, job-posting site. This means you've got to learn how to play the LinkedIn game. According to an article in *U.S. News & World Report*, a 2014 Jobvite survey of 2,135 adults found that 94 percent of recruiters use LinkedIn to source and vet candidates.[19]

The completeness of your profile has a direct impact on your visibility with prospective employers. For example, your profile is 23 times more likely to be viewed by adding your city and metro area, and 17 times more likely to be viewed if you add your education.[20] This chapter covers tips for maximizing the effectiveness of your LinkedIn profile.

Keywords

Your LinkedIn profile needs to illustrate to a recruiter or hiring manager that you have the requisite skills, talent, and experience for the job they are filling. How do you do that?

You must include the keywords relevant to the position you want in your LinkedIn profile.

Trudy Steinfeld, associate vice president and executive director of New York University's Wasserman Center for Career Development, also stresses the importance of using the right keywords, because that's how "applicant tracking systems and LinkedIn work. You have to use those exact same words to beat it."[21] Look for any descriptive word that has been used more than three times in the job posting. In addition, review the preferred skill sets section of the job opening. Many times keywords are included in that section.

Groups and Organizations

It is important to search your LinkedIn connections for people who are influencers in your industry. This can be as easy as starting a business conversation—not a job conversation—that shows off your business acumen. Steinfeld recommends joining relevant groups and following people on LinkedIn who are connected to your career interests.[10] This allows you to comment on relevant topics in public forums, which may get you attention from the influencers you are seeking.

It is important to join a large number of professional groups related to your skills and industry. For example, if you are a project manager in Chicago, do a search for project managers in the greater Chicago area. Many jobs are not publicly posted and you will only get access to them if you are a member of that professional group. It's also important to follow companies in your industry. The algorithms contained within LinkedIn recommend more influencers for you to connect with based on the number of groups you are associated with. The more professional groups and companies you follow, the more likely you are to get introduced to industry gatekeepers in your area. If you've developed multiple relationships over time with the right people, they will come to you with these job openings.

According to an article in LinkedIn, "There are over three million Company Pages on LinkedIn, so follow the ones you want to do business with…You'll get updates when people leave or join the company and you'll also get notified when that company posts jobs. LinkedIn Company Pages also show you if any of your contacts know people who work at those companies."[22]

LinkedIn Groups are incredible resources that can help you ramp up your job search quickly. By joining groups relevant to your profession or industry, you'll show that you're well connected and up to speed on trends within the industry. In addition, you'll instantly be connected to people and be included in relevant discussions in your field—kind of like an ongoing, online networking event.

Generally speaking there are three types of groups you want to join. The first type should be your prospective employer's industries. The next type is geographically-related groups like your local Chamber of Commerce. The final type should be based on your job title (CFO, project manager, computer programmer, etc.). Finding any of these groups is as easy as clicking on the search box at the top of the LinkedIn site and typing in the type or name of the group you are looking to find.

Profile Picture

It is important to have a professional headshot photo for your LinkedIn profile. Generally, recruiters will not spend time on your LinkedIn profile if you don't have a profile picture. According to LinkedIn, profiles that include a photo are 21 times more likely to be viewed than those without one.[20] Make sure you have a professional profile photo, be sure to use a neutral background for the picture, and wear business formal attire for most industries. It's worth paying a professional photographer to make your photo look more professional.

The more recent the photo, the better. Some people leave their profile picture up for years. When you're setting up a meeting for coffee or an interview, you want to be the person the other person has seen in your profile photo, not someone who looks vastly different. Your LinkedIn profile picture should be no more than 3 years old and be an accurate representation of what you look like now.

Custom URL

Nothing says, I am a LinkedIn amateur like having a URL like this: http://linkedin.com/pub/firstname-lastname435564-hjfjrigjhot.

It's important to clean up your LinkedIn URL by deleting the extra numbers and letters in it. When you first create your LinkedIn profile you are assigned a random cocktail of alpha numeric characters. Take the time to update your LinkedIn URL; it will make your profile easier to find by recruiters if you update it to a more searchable address. It's also much easier to publicize your profile with a customized URL (ideally www.linkedin.com/in/yourname).

How do you customize your LinkedIn URL? On the **Edit Profile** screen at the bottom of the gray window that shows your basic information, you'll see a Public Profile URL. Click **Edit** next to the URL and specify what you'd like your address to be. When you're finished, click **Set Custom URL.** If your name is already taken, include the first character of your first name and your last name, or add your professional title or a certification, or both. For example mine is www.linkedin.com/in/ryanandersonphd.

Professional Summary

Your professional summary is an important part of your LinkedIn profile. It should be a brief outline of your professional experience and skills, containing three to five short paragraphs, preferably with a bulleted section in the middle. The summary should quickly identify your work passions, key skills, and unique qualifications. Recruiters often scan profiles rapidly, so it is imperative that yours is a polished representation of your digital elevator pitch. You are more likely to turn up in a future employer's search if your summary is 40 words or more. Make sure that your professional summary includes many of the key buzzwords that recruiters will be searching for.

Endorsements

Another important aspect of your LinkedIn profile is seeking out endorsements from current and past co-workers and supervisors. Endorsements can be a great way to show off your skills—as long as your profile isn't overloaded with too many—and send the right message. It is important to keep your endorsements list current; review it every six months or so to ensure it's still accurate. As you transition between careers, develop new skills, or take on new responsibilities, drop outdated skills from your profile and add the ones you want to be known for. When people review your profile, they'll only see the most relevant skills.

Be specific about the skills that have made you successful in the work environment. If you don't include your best skills in your profile, you might fail to show up in a search when other professionals are looking for an expert just like you.

Connections

It's important to connect with as many people as possible on LinkedIn because LinkedIn is not like Facebook or Instagram; you don't have to be as selective in who you connect to. It is okay to reach out to people on LinkedIn who are only professional acquaintances—that is what is intended. You do not need to be lifelong friends to become connected on LinkedIn and the more exposure you have, the better.

If you are interested in working for a company, it's all right to locate people who work there and request an informational meeting. Invite them out for coffee or lunch and ask about the company's culture. Be sure to be up front on your reason for reaching out. Candor is key when making these kinds of requests. According to a LinkedIn article, "Family, friends, colleagues and peers are all valuable connections, but don't just send out a cold call to your inbox, it won't make you many friends. When requesting to connect, keep it personal instead of the standard message LinkedIn can send—it helps forge a relationship."[22]

If you have fewer than 100 connections on LinkedIn, recruiters assume one of three things: you are a recluse who knows very few people, you're paranoid about connecting with others, or technology and social media are scary to you. None of these are good. It is important to reach out via LinkedIn to at least 100 people for connections. LinkedIn has a function where you can import your email contacts and it can make suggestions for who you should connect with.

Privacy Settings

Your current job status should dictate how much or little you disclose about actively looking for another job. It is important to keep your job search discrete and it's generally a best practice to not advertise that you are on a job search. That situation changes if you are currently unemployed; some career coaches advise people to change their title to reflect that they are searching for a position. For example, their profile may say, "Project Manager seeking new opportunities." However, beware: once you update your LinkedIn profile title, recruiters will start reaching out to you and many of them are focused on sales opportunities. If that isn't a position you are interested in, advertising on LinkedIn that you are seeking a new job may not be a wise choice.

Many people don't realize that LinkedIn has privacy settings—for a reason. A telltale sign to an employer that you're leaving is to overhaul your profile, connect with recruiters, and have an influx of new connections. It's important to update your privacy settings so your current boss doesn't know you are actively searching for a new job. You can tailor your settings so your boss doesn't see that you're looking for opportunities. Just sign in and select **Settings & Privacy** from the drop-down menu where your name appears in the upper right-hand corner. The next step is to click on **Privacy** at the top of the screen. The last step is to click on **Sharing profile edits** and change it to No. This will ensure that everyone in your network is not needlessly notified when you update your profile.

Recommendations

Many people confuse the endorsements section on LinkedIn with the recommendations section. These different sections are both critical pieces of a successful profile. The endorsements section is a comprehensive list of your professional skills and characteristics. The recommendations section should include current or previous co-workers' and supervisors' thoughts on your professional abilities. The default setting in LinkedIn tells you that your profile is complete after receiving three recommendations. Most career coaches suggest having between five and ten good recommendations. When you request recommendations, provide a bulleted list of your skills, strengths, and services so people will write a more accurate account of how well you performed your job and not say something generic like, "She's good at what she does". It is also recommended that you write a recommendation for those who complete one on your behalf.

LinkedIn is a powerful and necessary resource for today's fast-paced job market. More and more recruiters are using it as a tool to find the most talented people. It's not enough to just have a nominal profile with partial information; it's important to ensure that you have a complete and accurate profile, including a profile statement, professional-looking picture, endorsements, and recommendations. Remember to follow a number of groups and companies, to increase your visibility. By following the tips listed in this chapter you will stand out to recruiters.

Discussion Questions:

1. What are three things you can do to improve your LinkedIn profile?

2. What are the advantages of changing your privacy settings within LinkedIn?

3. What strategy should you use when searching for companies and groups on LinkedIn to follow?

4. What types of people should you connect with on LinkedIn?

Exercises:

1. Research several LinkedIn profile pictures of people in your industry then have someone take a professional-looking photo for your LinkedIn profile.

2. Make sure you are following at least ten companies and groups within LinkedIn, preferably companies and industries that you are targeting for your job search.

3. Secure a minimum of ten recommendations from previous co-workers and supervisors.

4. Customize your LinkedIn profile URL. If your name is already taken, customize the URL to include your professional title.

CHAPTER 8
Nailing the Interview

"I sometimes find that in interviews you learn more about yourself than the person learned about you."
-William Shatner, Actor and Author

Now that you have submitted your polished resume and created a top tier LinkedIn profile, it is time to prepare for the all-important call from a recruiter. Your resume helps get your foot in the door, but how you present yourself in an interview is a make-or-break situation. It is your responsibility to convince the interviewer that you can do the job. Being prepared for an interview is key to convincing the hiring manager that you are the right candidate for the job. Interview preparation is not rocket science and by following some basic rules you can greatly increase your odds of nailing the interview. According to the book, *48 Days To The Work You Love*, "The word interview is derived from a Latin word that means "to see about each other." It is important to keep this definition in mind when interviewing."[17] The interview should be a two-way street that includes a mutual exchange of information. Most hiring decisions are made within the first five minutes of an interview. First impressions are lasting and this chapter will help you maximize your success by helping you put your best professional self forward. This chapter is organized into three sections: before the interview, during the interview, and after the interview.

BEFORE THE INTERVIEW

Research the Company You are Interviewing With

One of the best ways to have a great job interview is to study the company and review its mission and vision statements. Doing this gives you an idea of what the organization values. However, don't just memorize the statements from the company's website; figure out how your personal values line up with the company's values and be able to articulate that. The more you know about the company and what it stands for, the better your chance at building rapport with the interviewer. According to an article on Monster.com, "Learning as much as possible about its services, products, customers and competition will give you an edge in understanding and addressing the company's needs."[23]

You also should find out about the company's culture, to gain insight into your potential happiness on the job. Find out a minimum of three facts about the company; for example, a recent positive media headline, the location of its headquarters, and its mission and/or vision statement. Being able to discuss these items shows the interviewer that you have done your homework and that you have a genuine interest in the organization.

Know Thyself

As a candidate you should know your resume like the back of your hand; if it's included in your application papers, you are responsible for knowing everything it contains. In any job interview, anything on your resume is free game. Speaking intelligently about each of your previous positions and how they relate to the role you're interviewing for gives the employer confidence that they have the right person. Print a copy of your resume and take it with you just in case they ask you a question about a previous experience that you can't quickly answer.

Arrive Early

Drive by the interview location at least once before your scheduled appointment and be there about 20 minutes before the interview time. You don't want to risk showing up even a few minutes late—why risk missing an interview that could change your life? Sometimes traffic and weather can delay your commute to the interview, so plan on having at least 20 minutes before walking in, to gather your thoughts and run through a few last-minute, possible questions.

While it is clear why running late or cutting it close are not good strategies, the same goes for walking into the office more than 20 minutes early. Not every organization has a huge lobby or waiting area, or even a receptionist. If they do have a receptionist, she may not appreciate having to keep you company. Arriving too early might also make the interviewer think you are over eager and desperate for the job.

Dress to Impress

Many people forget to dress the part when going to a job interview. That's why doing your research and finding out about the company's culture is so important. If you are interviewing for a line job in a manufacturing plant, it may be appropriate to wear casual or business casual attire. If you are applying for a research analyst job at a Fortune 500 company, you should wear business formal attire to the interview.

According to an article in *USA Today*, Harvard professor and social psychologist Amy Cuddy reports that humans are judged on two primary factors: trustworthiness and respectability. Creating an ideal image does not require expensive outfits. It means selecting clothing, accessories, makeup, and a hairstyle that commands respect in your targeted industry.[24] It is important to pay attention to the details of your attire as well as making sure your clothes are stain and wrinkle free.

What Should You Bring to the Interview?

Bring at least two pens or pencils, a notebook or portfolio with paper, copies of your resume, and a list of questions you would like to ask the interviewer. Even though applications are submitted online, it's important to have a paper copy ready because many interviewers still ask for them. Providing a crisp, hard copy of your resume helps establish your competence and preparedness in the eyes of the recruiting manager.

During the Interview

Professional Examples

Being able to provide explicit examples to questions is a key aspect to a good interview. It is one thing to say you can do something; it's more impressive to give specific examples of things you have done that highlight your successes and uniqueness. Employers make the assumption that past performance is indicative of future results.

One of the biggest complaints made by hiring managers is when a candidate can't give explicit answers; they appear to be all talk and no substance. Candidates who can specifically cite examples tend to do better in interviews than those who just give vague answers. Evaluating the job description ahead of the interview for the required and preferred skills is a great place to start. Locate the top desired traits for the job and prepare strong and concise examples that clearly demonstrate how your experience and abilities match them.

It is very important to anticipate the questions a recruiter may ask. Think of recent strong examples of work you've done. Be sure each example you provide has a specific solution to the proposed situation or problem the question is inferring. Here is an example of some behavioral-based questions or requests.

1. Tell me about how you worked effectively under pressure.

2. How do you handle a challenge? Give an example.

3. Give an example of a goal you reached and tell me how you achieved it.

4. Give an example of how you worked on a team.

5. Have you handled a difficult situation? How?

6. Describe a time when you had to interact with a difficult client. What was the situation, and how did you handle it?

7. Describe a time when your team or company was undergoing a change. How did that impact you and how did you adapt?

8. Give me an example of a time you managed numerous responsibilities. How did you handle them?

9. Give me an example of a time when you were able to successfully persuade someone to see things your way at work.

10. Tell me about a time you were dissatisfied in your work. What could have been done to make it better?

Honesty is the Best Policy

It's never a good idea to exaggerate during an interview or on your resume; the lie always catches up with you at some point. Being candid about your strengths and weaknesses will get you ahead in the long run. Some candidates try to dance around difficult interview questions. Don't do this. Instead, try to figure out what exactly the interviewer is asking you. According to an article on Monster.com, "Make sure you understand what is being asked, and get further clarification if you are unsure. If you don't have a skill, just state it. Don't try to cover it up by talking and giving examples that aren't relevant. You're much better off saying you don't have that skill, but perhaps you do have some related skills, and you're happy to tell them about that if they like."[23]

Be Conversational

The best interviews tend to involve conversations instead of a very formal question and answer session. It is important to come prepared to discuss the following items: company mission and values, the job opportunity, your professional and educational background, the reason for the opening, and any recent business events that may impact the interviewer, role, company, or industry. Recruiters are looking to hire engaged people who have taken the time to learn about the company and position they are applying for.

Unfortunately, most interviews can quickly become one-sided exchanges in which the interviewer asks questions and the candidate responds to the question. Making small talk in this type of stressful situation can be a critical skill that leads to a job offer. The ability to have fluid discussions conveys preparation, intelligence, people skills, active listening, and a commitment to your career. Being conversational in the interview environment puts you at the top of the list.

Take Notes

It is important to take notes during the interview; that is where the notepad comes in handy. This shows the hiring manager that you are both interested and paying attention during the interview process. Job seekers should bring a padfolio to interviews and stock it full of copies of their resumes; a resume should be given to everyone they meet during their interviews. Notes taken should focus on the kind of questions interviewers are asking, and points to be followed up on post-interview. Key nuggets of information should be captured that you can use after the interview, for instance, it's best not to find yourself a week later referring to the wrong company name or calling the hiring agent by the wrong name.

Final Questions and Interview Wrap Up

Closing the interview strongly is key and may be one of the most important pieces of the whole process. How you close the interview dictates how the employer feels about you. One way to close strongly is to ask the interviewer two or three questions. Some examples are:

- What is an average day in this position like?

- How would you describe the departmental/corporate culture?

- What is your favorite part of working here?

- What are the next steps in the hiring process?

It's also important to avoid asking any negative-sounding questions such as: How many hours a week do people work here? Do you like your boss?

According to an article on Monster.com, "The questions you ask indicate your interest in the company or job. He says nothing impresses him more than a really good question that not only shows you've researched the company in general, but also the specific job you're hoping to land in particular. That makes me go, 'Wow, this person has really done their homework.' "[12]

Always remember, you are interviewing the company just as much as they are interviewing you. Ask questions that give you a better understanding about whether the company is what you are looking for. Always finish the interview by asking what the next steps are; then declare your interest in the company and the opportunity.

Follow-up Etiquette

Following up properly after the interview is just as significant as doing well while interviewing. According to an article on *Business Insider*, "How you handle the post-interview process is just as important as how you performed during the actual interview," says Amanda Augustine, a career-advice expert for TopResume. "I know clients who point-blank were told they didn't get the job because they didn't follow up after the interview," she says. "Don't be that person!"[25]

Just following up isn't enough; you need to do it correctly. Here are some tricks of the trade that will help you professionally follow up after the interview.

- Before you leave the interview ask two very important questions.

  o What is the timeline for making the hiring decision?

  o When and with whom should I follow up?

- Get that person's contact information; ask for a business card of every person you meet with during the interview.

It's important to send a follow up e-mail within a short period of time; 48 hours is recommended.

Securing an interview is a significant accomplishment; winning a great interview takes a lot of preparation and research. It is important to research not only the job description, but also the company's website, to make sure you can speak about its core mission and vision statement. It is important to arrive early, dress in the appropriate attire, and bring a notebook, pens, and copies of your resume. During the interview do your best to be both informed and conversational. Have specific examples of your professional background that speak to the needs of the job opening. Come prepared with some questions for the end of the interview. Make the most of each job opportunity by incorporating these tips into your interview strategy.

Discussion Questions:

1. What are three things you can research in advance of the interview?

2. What kind of questions should you have prepared for the interview?

3. What strategy should you use when developing examples for various interview questions?

4. What items should you bring to the interview?

Exercises:

1. Research the company's website for their mission and vision statement. Think of ways to work your findings into the interview.

2. Write down four or five of the most important core competencies from the job description. Prepare examples of how your experience meets those core competencies for the interview.

3. Practice driving to the location of the interview. Be sure to show up at least 20 minutes early.

4. Research the company to find out about appropriate attire. Select an outfit for the interview that fits the culture of the organization.

CHAPTER 9

Follow-Up Etiquette

"If I don't get a thank you note, I assume the person doesn't want the job, is disorganized, and I'll likely forget about them."

- Jessica Liebman, Managing Editor, Business Insider (2016)

At this point you have a high-profile resume, an awesome LinkedIn profile, and have nailed the interview process. Now comes the closer: how to follow up with a killer thank you. This chapter walks you through some best practices for following up after the interview is over.

Hiring agents expect you to follow up with a thank you. Failure to follow up could leave the impression that you are not interested enough to go the extra mile and reach out afterward. An article on TheLadders.com states, "A study by Ladders found more than 75 percent of interviewers say receiving a thank-you note impacts their decision-making process."[26] A good thank you note shows not only that you are interested in the position, but also indicates why you are the best candidate for the job. Chances are you won't land the job based on your thank you note, but you might not get a job if you don't send one. Not sending a thank you is a surefire way to not be seriously considered.

Recap Highlights of the Interview

When crafting a high-quality thank you note start by recapping some of the best moments from the interview. If there were any awkward moments during the interview, this can be a good time to address them. It's not necessary to draw attention to minor mistakes, but if there were any major mistakes the thank you note is your opportunity to bring it up and provide an explanation.

Personalize Your Thank You Note

It is important to customize every thank you note for every person you interviewed with. They will compare notes, so no two thank you notes should be the same. Every communication should have a specific purpose. It should include thanking them for their time, expressing continued interest in the position, and citing a specific part of the interview that impressed you. Everyone will have a slightly different take on your interaction because every interviewer will ask different interview questions; that can help you personalize your thank you.

According to an article on TheMuse.com, "But there's a difference between a generic note and a tailored one—the latter makes the recipient feel far more special, which in turn creates a much more effective letter. This is especially true if it's a thank you note for an interview where several employees asked you similar questions. You obviously can't write the same note to all of them."[27] That is why it's so important to send an individual note to all interviewers.

Handwritten Versus Email Thank You

It is important to send your thank you note in the appropriate medium. The majority of times an email will suffice, but there are occasions when a handwritten thank you note will stand out. For candidates who are wondering whether it's appropriate to send a handwritten note instead of an email, there's no easy answer to this question. Although a handwritten note may offer a unique opportunity, the organization will likely receive it too late for it to have an impact on the hiring decision. Here are some rules on when to handwrite a thank you note:

- If you had just an initial interview and there will be more rounds of interviews, an email will suffice.

- If you interviewed face to face at a more traditional organization (i.e. insurance company), consider sending a thank you note by mail in addition to an email.

- If you're interviewing with a technology company, only send an email.

- If there will be two to three weeks until a hiring decision is made, you can send a handwritten thank you note that first week.

Sending a LinkedIn Follow Up

It's recommended that you also send a LinkedIn connection request a day or two after you email your thank you note. According to an article on *Business Insider*, "Your personal message must be 300 characters or less, so it should concisely express your gratitude for your interviewer's time and your interest in the role.

For example:

It was a pleasure meeting you and learning more about your responsibilities at [COMPANY] and the marketing manager position.

I'm very interested in joining your team. Please don't hesitate to reach out, should you have any questions.

In the meantime, I'd like to add you to my LinkedIn network.

Best,

[Name]"[28]

Using LinkedIn can also help you find some great connecting points with your interviewers. Reading through their professional summaries and past employers can quickly help you glean things that you have in common with them. "There's usually some great letter fodder in your connections' summaries. Maybe the professional I'm writing to was born and raised in Ireland; I'll add a line like, "I noticed on your LinkedIn you grew up in Ireland. I love it there—do you get the chance to go back often?"[27]

Timing of Thank You Notes

Another important topic when it comes to writing a thank you note is the timing of following up. A recent CareerBliss.com poll inquired about how soon people follow up after a job interview; 39 percent of respondents said they do it the next day.[30] The timing and frequency of follow up should depend on how the interview went and the feedback you received from the interviewer during it.

- You should pace your follow ups with the timeline you asked for after your interview. If they said it would take less than a week to make a decision, send an email the next day.

- One thank you email is appropriate, along with one additional follow-up email a few days later, to check on the status of the opening.

- According to an article on *Business Insider*, "If your potential employer never provided you with specific information about following up, a good rule of thumb is to follow up approximately one week after you send your thank you note."[28] Remember, there's a fine line between being enthusiastic and annoying a recruiter. Don't come off as desperate.

When following up with the recruiter or hiring manager via email you should ask the following questions:

- Where are you in the hiring process?

- How do my credentials compare against the other candidates?

- Can you think of any reason why you would be reluctant to hire me versus one of the other candidates?

Length

Many follow up notes are long and tiring. It's important to be concise and not use unnecessary language in your follow-up message. According to an article on WorkItDaily.com, "Generally, a good rule of thumb for the length is three paragraphs, with no more than two to three sentences in each paragraph."[30] Here is a general outline of how your thank you note should flow.

- **First Paragraph:** Briefly thank them for their time and restate your interest in the position.

- **Second Paragraph:** Discuss a couple of your strengths and how the company would benefit if you were hired. Consider using bullet points to break up your text.

- **Third Paragraph:** Include any points of explanation you might have, such as answers to questions that you weren't able to answer during the interview, or new information about yourself that was left out of the interview. Remember, keep it brief.

This format will keep you on track and ensure you have the best possible follow-up note. The flow will help you stand out in a crowded field of job applicants.

Know Your Audience

It's important to know your intended audience while crafting your thank you note. Put yourself in the mindset of the people who interviewed you: what will they want to read? Here are three primary points to include in your letter.

- Thank the person for meeting with you

- Mention something you liked about the interview

- Repeat your interest in the job

It's important to write a nice, polished letter. Don't be too casual or laid back with your wording and don't use emoticons or write like you text. Try to avoid using acronyms and shorthand.

Common Mistakes

Many job searchers are so rushed to send out thank you notes that they make obvious mistakes. It is important to review your thank you at least three times before you send it out. Here are some common mistakes to avoid.

- Repetition

- Negativity

- Gossip or rumors

- Excessive exclamation points

- Informal language

- Grammar/spelling errors

By using these basic follow-up techniques you will be more likely to get a job offer. It is important to consider your follow up as a strategic part of your job search process. A polished follow-up message can give you just the edge you need to get the job offer over others who interviewed for the position. Use these follow-up techniques to continue to show your enthusiasm and desire for the position, but don't make it sound as if you are desperate. Remember the analogy about the squeaky wheel getting the grease, but do not go overboard and irritate the hiring manager. Here is a sample thank you letter.

Dear Mr. Jones,

Thank you for taking the time to discuss the insurance broker position at Big Time Investments with me. After meeting with you and observing the company's operations, I am further convinced that my background and skills coincide well with your needs.

I really appreciate that you took so much time to acquaint me with the company. It became obvious to me during the interview why employees have such long tenure at your organization.

In addition to my education, qualifications, and experience, I will bring an excellent work ethic to this position. With the countless demands on your time, I am sure that you require people who can be trusted to carry out their responsibilities with minimal supervision.

Mr. Jones, I look forward to hearing from you concerning your hiring decision. Again, thank you for your time and consideration.

Sincerely,

Ryan Anderson

Discussion Questions:

1. What is the appropriate length of a follow-up email?

2. When can you handwrite a thank you note?

3. Why is it so important to personalize your note to each interviewer?

4. How long should you wait to follow up with the hiring manager?

Exercises:

1. Research three blog posts about what should go into a good thank you note.

2. Review your interview notes and use them to create a customized thank you note for each interviewer.

3. Create follow-up reminders to send your thank you notes within 24 hours following the interview.

4. Use LinkedIn to find some great connecting points to each interviewer and send a connection request to each one.

CHAPTER 10

Final Thoughts

"Whenever you are asked if you can do a job, tell 'em,
'Certainly I can!' Then get busy and find out how to do it."
—*Theodore Roosevelt, President of the United States*

A.B.C.: always be closing! Finding a job is all about closing, which is a sales term. Every sales representative must close, or they may lose that business. The job interview is a sales process and the process is a two-way street. You are trying to sell yourself to the employer and they are trying to sell you on the company culture. This chapter provides a variety of tips on how to effectively start and close strong during the job search.

The processes laid out in this book will help you find your true life's calling in a deliberate, effective fashion. These include creating top tier cover and thank you letters, crafting a polished and concise resume, practicing your interview skills, keeping organized during the job search, and using LinkedIn, Glassdoor, and other online technology to make your search more efficient. It is important to always be networking and to maintain an updated, professional LinkedIn profile while on the job search. Here are some final tips and thoughts on the job search.

1. Finding a job is one part science (technology and Applicant Tracking System) and one part art (networking).

2. It is imperative to be actively networking in groups while on your job search. Pick one or two local groups to join based on demographics (young professionals) or industry (accounting).

3. Create multiple job queries on Indeed and research prospective companies on Glassdoor.

4. Write a customized cover letter using keywords from the job description for every different application.

5. Customize the professional summary and core competency section of your resume for each job opening.

6. Complete your LinkedIn profile with a professional summary, recommendations, and endorsements. Be sure to follow, and participate in, multiple professional groups and organizations on LinkedIn.

7. Write a quick and succinct thank you letter within 48 hours of the interview. Then follow up a few days later with an email to your contact in the organization.

8. Develop a system to help you stay organized during your job search, with spreadsheets, a calendar, and a separate email account for your job search.

Following the best practices in this book will help you efficiently search out and find the best jobs available.

Technology can be your friend, but you must constantly check for updated job openings during the process. Time management is an important skill in finding a job because looking for a job is time consuming and challenging, even in the best of job markets. By using the content in this book you can quickly and strategically find the job you have always wanted. The job of your dreams is closer than you think. Don't wait; get started today!

Bibliography

1. Adkins, A. (2016, January 13). *Employee engagement in U.S. stagnant in 2015*. Retrieved from http://www.gallup.com/poll/188144/employee-engagement-stagnant-2015.aspx.

2. Gimbel, T. (2017, April 4). *4 types of bad bosses and how to deal with them*. Retrieved from http://fortune.com/2017/04/04/leadership-career-advice-bad-boss-office-space-work-relationships.

3. *Job* [Def. 1,2,3]. (2017, August). In Dictionary.com. Retrieved from http://www.dictionary.com/browse/job.

4. *Career* [Def. 1,2,3]. (2017, August). In Dictionary.com. Retrieved from http://www.dictionary.com/browse/career.

5. Glassdoor Team. (2016, July 22). *How job seekers are using Glassdoor.* Retrieved from https://www.glassdoor.com/employers/blog/how-candidates-use-glassdoor.

6. Charney, M. (2014, January 28). *How job seekers really use Glassdoor reviews.* Retrieved from http://recruitingdaily.com/glassdoor-reviews.

7. *How technology is changing the job search.* (2015, July 21). Retrieved from http://www.rightmanagement.ca/wps/wcm/connect/right-ca-en/home/thoughtwire/categories/career-work/How-Technology-is-Changing-the-Job-Search.

8. Adler, L. (2016, February 29). *New survey reveals 85% of all jobs are filled via networking.* Retrieved from https://www.linkedin.com/pulse/new-survey-reveals-85-all-jobs-filled-via-networking-lou-adler.

9. Doyle, A. (2017, June 22). *The importance of career networking.* Retrieved from

https://www.thebalance.com/top-career-networking-tips-2062604.

10. Olson, L. (2011, October 18). *6 networking tips for your job search*. Retrieved from https://money.usenews.com/money/blogs/outside-voices-careers/2011/10/18/6-networking-tips-for-your-job-search.

11. Appelbaum, D. (2016, June 29). *Networking advice*. Retrieved from https://www.linkedin.com/pulse/networking-advice-doris-appelbaum.

12. Evans, W. (2012, March 12). *You have 6 seconds to make an impression: How recruiters see your resume*. Retrieved from https://www.theladders.com/p/10541/you-only-get-6-seconds-of-fame-make-it-count.

13. McCord, S. (n.d.). *This simple formula makes highlighting transferable skills easy*. Retrieved from

https://www.themuse.com/advice/this-simple-formula-makes-highlighting-transferable-skills-easy.

14.   Yeager, M. (2015, December 3). *How job hunting has changed in the last decade.* Retrieved from https://money.usnews.com/money/blogs/outside-voices-careers/2015/12/03/how-job-hunting-has-changed-in-the-last-decade.

15.   Doyle, A. (2017, May 1). *How often do people change jobs?* Retrieved from https://www.thebalance.com/how-often-do-people-change-jobs-2060467.

16.   Stahl, A. (2015, June 11). *The cover letter is (almost) dead.* Retrieved from https://www.forbes.com/sites/ashleystahl/2015/06/11/the-cover-letter-is-almost-dead/#57bcf4975237.

17.   Miller, D. (2015). *48 Days To The Work You Love.* Nashville, TN: B&H Publishing Group.

18.   Hansen, K. (n.d.). *The scoop on resume length: How many pages should your resume be?* Retrieved from

https://www.livecareer.com/quintessential/resume-length.

19. McMullen, L. (2015, February 19). *What recruiters think when they see your LinkedIn profile: And how to impress the heck out of them.* Retrieved from https://money.usnews.com/money/careers/articles/2015/02/19/what-recruiters-think-when-they-see-your-linkedin-profile.

20. Ward, M. (2017, March 27). *7 LinkedIn hacks that will help you get noticed by recruiters.* Retrieved from https://www.cnbc.com/2017/03/27/7-linkedin-hacks-that-will-help-you-get-noticed-by-recruiters.html.

21. Petrow, S. (2017, March 24). *How to use LinkedIn to find your dream job.* Retrieved from https://www.msn.com/en-us/money/careersandeducation/how-to-use-linkedin-to-find-your-dream-job/ar-BByGyp3.

22. Talalweh, B. (2016, May 23). *13 ways you can use your LinkedIn profile to get your dream job read.* Retrieved from https://www.linkedin.com/pulse/13-ways-you-can-use-your-linkedin-profile-get-dream-job-talalweh.

23. Martin, C. (n.d.). *Ten interviewing rules.* Retrieved from https://www.monster.ca/career-advice/article/ten-interview-rules-ca.

24. Reshwan, R. (2017, June 19). *5 expert tips for interview success: While it is important to be qualified, it is even more important to create the right impression.* Retrieved from https://money.usnews.com/money/blogs/outside-voices-careers/articles/2017-06-19/5-expert-tips-for-interview-success.

25. Gillet, R. (2017, June 13). *Everything you should do in the minutes, hours, days, and weeks following a job interview.* Retrieved from. http://www.businessinsider.com/what-you-should-do-after-a-job-interview-2017-6.

26. Augustine, A. (2014, November 25). *Give thanks after each job interview with these tips*. Retrieved from https://www.theladders.com/p/1456/interview-thank-you-email-5-tips.

27. Frost, A. (n.d.). *4 ways to give your follow-up letter a personal touch (and make the recipient feel warm & fuzzy*. Retrieved from https://www.themuse.com/advice/4-ways-to-give-your-followup-letter-a-personal-touch-and-make-the-recipient-feel-warm-fuzzy.

28. Gillet, R. (2016, June 28). *13 things you should do after a job interview*. Retrieved from http://www.businessinsider.com/what-you-should-do-after-a-job-interview-2016-6.

29. CareerBliss. (2015, July 23). *6 tips for following up after a job interview*. Retrieved from https://www.workitdaily.com/job-interview-following-up.

 Dr. Anderson earned his doctorate in Educational Leadership and Policy Studies from Iowa State University in Ames, IA. He also has a Master's in Business Administration from Drake University in Des Moines, IA. He spent several years working in the financial services industry for several Fortune 500 companies including Hewlett Packard, Principal and Standard and Poors (McGraw Hill).

He has spent the last seven years as Business Professor at Grand View University in Des Moines, IA. His areas of specialization include financial literacy, investments, strategic management and career coaching.

In his free time he enjoys spending time with wife and two young boys and all things related to the Iowa Hawkeyes.

Dr. Anderson is a speaker, professor, business and career coach. He started a consulting business to help mentor those looking to make a career change. Dr. Anderson is a dynamic speaker able to present on a variety of career related topics from resume creation, LinkedIn profiles, interview coaching and much more.

If you are interested in learning more about Dr. Anderson's business, No Coast Consulting, or inquiring about him as a speaker please visit nocoastconsulting.com.

79607528R00090

Made in the USA
Lexington, KY
24 January 2018